EMMANUEL JOSEPH

Pioneers of Prosperity, Human Insights from Silicon Valley and Real Estate Leaders

Copyright © 2025 by Emmanuel Joseph

All rights reserved. No part of this publication may be reproduced, stored or transmitted in any form or by any means, electronic, mechanical, photocopying, recording, scanning, or otherwise without written permission from the publisher. It is illegal to copy this book, post it to a website, or distribute it by any other means without permission.

First edition

*This book was professionally typeset on Reedsy.
Find out more at reedsy.com*

Contents

1	Chapter 1	1
2	Chapter 1: The Dawn of Silicon Valley	3
3	Chapter 2: The Visionaries Behind Tech Giants	5
4	Chapter 3: The Rise of Real Estate Titans	7
5	Chapter 4: Lessons in Leadership	9
6	Chapter 5: Innovating for the Future	11
7	Chapter 6: The Role of Culture in Success	13
8	Chapter 7: Strategies for Growth and Expansion	15
9	Chapter 8: The Impact of Technology on Real Estate	17
10	Chapter 9: Navigating Economic Cycles	19
11	Chapter 10: Sustainable and Ethical Practices	21
12	Chapter 11: The Future of Work	23
13	Chapter 12: The Legacy of Pioneers	25

1

Chapter 1

Introduction

Silicon Valley and the real estate industry are two of the most dynamic and influential sectors in the global economy. Both have shaped the way we live, work, and interact with the world around us. "Pioneers of Prosperity: Human Insights from Silicon Valley and Real Estate Leaders" delves into the lives and experiences of the visionaries who have driven these industries forward. Through their stories, we gain a deeper understanding of the qualities and strategies that have led to their success, as well as the challenges they have overcome along the way.

The tech industry, centered in Silicon Valley, is a testament to the power of innovation and entrepreneurship. From the early days of semiconductor pioneers to the rise of internet giants, Silicon Valley has been a breeding ground for groundbreaking ideas and transformative technologies. The region's unique ecosystem, characterized by a culture of risk-taking, collaboration, and diversity, has produced some of the most iconic companies and leaders in history. This book explores the personal journeys of these tech visionaries, shedding light on the mindset and values that have driven their achievements.

Similarly, the real estate industry has seen the rise of formidable leaders who have redefined urban landscapes and created iconic developments. These real estate titans have demonstrated exceptional strategic vision, negotiation skills, and a deep understanding of market dynamics. Their ability to identify opportunities, innovate, and navigate economic cycles has not only built their empires but also contributed to the growth and prosperity of communities. By examining their stories, we gain valuable insights into the principles and practices that underpin success in the real estate sector.

Throughout this book, we will explore the commonalities and differences between these two industries, highlighting the unique challenges and opportunities they present. From leadership and innovation to sustainability and ethics, the book provides a comprehensive analysis of the factors that drive success in both Silicon Valley and real estate. By drawing parallels and contrasts, we uncover the universal principles that can be applied across various fields to achieve prosperity.

Ultimately, "Pioneers of Prosperity" is not just a celebration of individual achievements but also an exploration of the collective impact these leaders have had on their industries and society. Their stories inspire us to think big, embrace innovation, and pursue excellence in our own endeavors. As we journey through the lives of these pioneers, we are reminded of the power of vision, resilience, and the relentless pursuit of progress. This book serves as a source of inspiration and guidance for aspiring entrepreneurs and leaders, offering timeless lessons that can shape our paths to success.

2

Chapter 1: The Dawn of Silicon Valley

The story of Silicon Valley is not just about groundbreaking technology; it's about visionary people. From the early days when the likes of Hewlett-Packard set up shop in a tiny garage, to the explosive growth driven by companies like Apple and Google, Silicon Valley has always been about innovation. It is a place where dreams become reality, often through relentless effort and an unwavering belief in the power of technology to change the world. The Valley's culture of risk-taking and failure as a stepping stone to success is what sets it apart. Here, failure is not the end but rather a learning experience that fuels future success.

Entrepreneurs in Silicon Valley have a unique mindset that combines technical expertise with business acumen. They are not just engineers but also visionaries who can foresee market needs and trends. This duality allows them to create products that not only solve problems but also appeal to the masses. This chapter delves into the lives of some of the early pioneers, exploring their backgrounds, motivations, and the challenges they overcame to build their empires.

Moreover, the ecosystem of Silicon Valley has always played a crucial role in its success. The close proximity of venture capital firms, tech startups, and academic institutions like Stanford University creates a fertile ground for innovation. This unique environment fosters collaboration and competition, driving the continuous evolution of technology. The chapter also highlights how this ecosystem supports entrepreneurs, providing them with the resources and network they need to succeed.

Another significant aspect of Silicon Valley's success is its diversity. The Valley attracts talent from all over the world, creating a melting pot of ideas and cultures. This diversity leads to innovative solutions and perspectives that might not emerge in a more homogenous environment. The chapter discusses how this blend of cultures contributes to the region's dynamism and ability to stay ahead of the curve.

Finally, this chapter examines the role of mentorship in Silicon Valley. Many successful entrepreneurs have mentors who guide them through the complexities of starting and running a business. These mentors provide invaluable advice, helping new entrepreneurs navigate the pitfalls and opportunities that come their way. The culture of giving back and supporting the next generation is a cornerstone of Silicon Valley's enduring success.

3

Chapter 2: The Visionaries Behind Tech Giants

The tech industry is replete with iconic figures whose visions have shaped the modern world. This chapter focuses on the personal journeys of some of these visionaries, such as Steve Jobs, Bill Gates, and Elon Musk. Their stories are not just about their companies but about their relentless pursuit of innovation and excellence. These leaders share a common trait: an unyielding belief in their ideas, even in the face of skepticism and setbacks.

Steve Jobs' journey with Apple exemplifies the power of perseverance and innovation. From founding the company in his garage to being ousted and then returning to lead one of the most remarkable turnarounds in corporate history, Jobs' story is a testament to the importance of vision and execution. His ability to blend technology with art and create products that resonate with consumers on an emotional level set Apple apart in the tech world.

Bill Gates' story with Microsoft is equally compelling. Gates' early recognition of the potential of personal computing and his strategic vision for software development propelled Microsoft to the forefront of the tech industry. His philanthropic efforts through the Bill & Melinda Gates Foundation also highlight his commitment to using his success to address global challenges, making a lasting impact beyond the tech world.

Elon Musk, the visionary behind companies like Tesla and SpaceX, represents the new wave of tech entrepreneurs who are not just focused on profits but on solving some of humanity's biggest challenges. Musk's ambition to revolutionize transportation and colonize Mars showcases the audacity and far-reaching impact of modern tech entrepreneurship. His story highlights the importance of thinking big and pushing the boundaries of what is possible.

The chapter also explores the commonalities among these visionaries, such as their leadership styles, decision-making processes, and the ability to inspire and motivate their teams. These leaders share an unwavering commitment to their missions, often working long hours and making significant personal sacrifices to achieve their goals. Their stories provide valuable insights into the qualities that define successful tech entrepreneurs.

Furthermore, this chapter delves into the lessons these visionaries have learned along the way. From navigating market changes to handling crises, their experiences offer a wealth of knowledge for aspiring entrepreneurs. The chapter emphasizes the importance of resilience, adaptability, and continuous learning in the journey to success in the tech industry.

4

Chapter 3: The Rise of Real Estate Titans

While Silicon Valley has garnered much attention for its technological innovations, the real estate industry has also produced its share of trailblazers. This chapter explores the journeys of real estate moguls who have transformed landscapes and created lasting legacies. Figures like Donald Trump, Barbara Corcoran, and Sam Zell have made indelible marks on the industry through their innovative approaches and strategic investments.

Donald Trump's rise in the real estate world is a story of ambition and tenacity. Despite facing numerous challenges and controversies, Trump built a real estate empire that includes some of the most iconic properties in the world. His ability to market and brand his properties set him apart from his peers, making him a household name in the real estate industry.

Barbara Corcoran's journey is a tale of perseverance and resilience. From starting her real estate business with a $1,000 loan to building one of the most successful real estate firms in New York City, Corcoran's story is an inspiration to aspiring entrepreneurs. Her emphasis on customer service and innovative marketing strategies helped her rise to the top of a highly competitive industry.

Sam Zell, known as the "Grave Dancer," made his mark by identifying undervalued assets and transforming them into profitable ventures. His contrarian approach to investing and his keen ability to spot opportunities in distressed properties have made him a legend in the real estate world. Zell's story highlights the importance of strategic thinking and the willingness to take calculated risks.

The chapter also examines the common traits among these real estate titans, such as their strategic vision, negotiation skills, and ability to identify and capitalize on market trends. These leaders share a relentless drive to succeed and a keen understanding of the intricacies of the real estate market. Their stories provide valuable insights into the qualities that define successful real estate entrepreneurs.

Additionally, this chapter explores the impact of these real estate moguls on their communities and the broader economy. Through their investments and developments, they have created jobs, revitalized neighborhoods, and contributed to economic growth. The chapter emphasizes the importance of responsible and sustainable development in the real estate industry.

5

Chapter 4: Lessons in Leadership

Effective leadership is a common thread that runs through the stories of successful entrepreneurs in both Silicon Valley and the real estate industry. This chapter delves into the leadership principles and practices that have propelled these pioneers to the pinnacle of their fields. From visionary thinking to empathetic management, the chapter explores the diverse leadership styles that drive innovation and growth.

Visionary thinking is a hallmark of successful leaders. Whether it's envisioning the future of technology or identifying emerging market trends, visionary leaders have the ability to see opportunities where others see challenges. This forward-thinking approach enables them to stay ahead of the competition and drive their companies toward long-term success. The chapter discusses how leaders cultivate this mindset and translate their vision into actionable strategies.

Empathy and emotional intelligence are also crucial components of effective leadership. Successful leaders understand the importance of building strong relationships with their teams, customers, and stakeholders. They create a supportive and inclusive work environment that fosters collaboration and innovation. The chapter highlights the role of empathy in leadership and provides examples of how leaders have used emotional intelligence to navigate challenges and drive positive outcomes.

Resilience is another key trait of successful leaders. The journey to success is often fraught with setbacks and obstacles. Resilient leaders have the ability to persevere in the face of adversity, adapt to changing circumstances, and maintain their focus on long-term goals. The chapter explores the importance of resilience and provides insights into how leaders build and sustain this quality.

Decision-making is a critical aspect of leadership. Successful leaders are adept at making informed and timely decisions, even under pressure. They gather relevant information, consider multiple perspectives, and weigh the potential risks and benefits before arriving at a decision. The chapter discusses the decision-making processes of successful leaders and provides examples of how they have navigated complex situations.

Furthermore, this chapter examines the role of mentorship and continuous learning in leadership. Many successful leaders have mentors who provide guidance and support throughout their careers. They also prioritize continuous learning and stay updated on industry trends and developments. The chapter emphasizes the importance of mentorship and lifelong learning in leadership development.

6

Chapter 5: Innovating for the Future

Innovation is at the heart of both Silicon Valley and the real estate industry. This chapter explores the innovative approaches and technologies that have revolutionized these fields. From cutting-edge software and hardware to groundbreaking architectural designs, the chapter delves into the innovations that are shaping the future.

In Silicon Valley, innovation is driven by a culture of experimentation and risk-taking. Tech companies are constantly pushing the boundaries of what is possible, developing new products and services that transform industries and improve lives. The chapter highlights some of the most significant technological innovations, such as artificial intelligence, blockchain, and renewable energy solutions, and discusses their potential impact on the future.

The real estate industry is also experiencing a wave of innovation. Advances in construction technology, smart home systems, and sustainable building practices are transforming the way properties are developed and managed. The chapter explores how real estate companies are leveraging these innovations to create more efficient, sustainable, and user-friendly spaces. It also discusses the role of technology in enhancing the buying and selling experience for consumers.

Collaboration and cross-industry partnerships are key drivers of innovation. Tech companies and real estate firms are increasingly working together to develop solutions that address complex challenges, such as urbanization, climate change, and housing affordability. The chapter provides examples of successful collaborations and discusses the benefits of combining expertise from different fields to drive innovation.

Moreover, the chapter discusses the role of innovation in addressing global challenges. From developing sustainable energy solutions to creating affordable housing, both tech companies and real estate firms are at the forefront of tackling some of the world's most pressing issues. The chapter highlights how innovation can drive positive change and create a better future for all.

7

Chapter 6: The Role of Culture in Success

Culture plays a pivotal role in the success of organizations. This chapter explores how the unique cultures of Silicon Valley and real estate firms contribute to their achievements. From fostering creativity and collaboration to promoting diversity and inclusion, the chapter delves into the cultural elements that drive success.

In Silicon Valley, the culture of innovation and risk-taking is ingrained in the DNA of tech companies. This culture encourages employees to think outside the box, experiment with new ideas, and embrace failure as a learning opportunity. The chapter discusses how this culture fosters a continuous cycle of innovation and growth, enabling companies to stay ahead of the competition.

The real estate industry also has its own unique culture. Successful real estate firms prioritize customer service, building long-term relationships, and creating value for their clients. The chapter explores how this customer-centric approach drives success in the real estate industry. It also highlights the importance of ethical practices and responsible development in building a positive reputation and achieving long-term success.

Diversity and inclusion are also crucial components of organizational culture. Both Silicon Valley and real estate firms recognize the value of diverse perspectives and backgrounds in driving innovation and growth. The chapter discusses how companies are fostering diversity and inclusion through various initiatives and creating an inclusive work environment where everyone feels valued and empowered.

Furthermore, this chapter examines the role of leadership in shaping organizational culture. Leaders set the tone for the culture of their organizations through their actions, values, and communication. The chapter provides examples of how leaders in both Silicon Valley and the real estate industry have created positive and high-performing cultures that drive success.

8

Chapter 7: Strategies for Growth and Expansion

Growth and expansion are essential for the long-term success of any organization. This chapter explores the strategies used by successful tech companies and real estate firms to grow and expand their businesses. From scaling operations to entering new markets, the chapter provides insights into the tactics and approaches that drive growth.

In Silicon Valley, growth is often driven by innovation and the ability to scale rapidly. Tech companies leverage their technological expertise and market insights to develop products and services that meet evolving customer needs. The chapter discusses how companies use data analytics, market research, and customer feedback to identify growth opportunities and make informed decisions.

Real estate firms also employ various strategies for growth and expansion. These strategies include identifying emerging markets, diversifying their portfolios, and leveraging technology to enhance efficiency and service delivery. The chapter explores how real estate firms use these strategies to achieve sustainable growth and create value for their clients and investors.

Strategic partnerships and collaborations are also key drivers of growth. Both tech companies and real estate firms recognize the benefits of partnering with other organizations to access new markets, share resources, and drive innovation. The chapter provides examples of successful partnerships and discusses the factors that contribute to their success.

Moreover, this chapter examines the challenges and risks associated with growth and expansion. From managing financial resources to navigating regulatory environments, organizations must carefully plan and execute their growth strategies to mitigate risks and achieve their goals. The chapter provides insights into how successful companies address these challenges and maintain a balance between growth and stability.

9

Chapter 8: The Impact of Technology on Real Estate

Technology is transforming the real estate industry in unprecedented ways. This chapter explores the impact of technological advancements on various aspects of real estate, from property development and management to marketing and transactions. The chapter discusses how technology is enhancing efficiency, transparency, and customer experience in the real estate industry.

Smart home technology is one of the most significant innovations in real estate. The integration of smart devices and systems into homes is transforming the way people live, making their lives more convenient, secure, and energy-efficient. The chapter explores how real estate firms are incorporating smart home technology into their developments and the benefits it offers to homeowners.

Virtual reality (VR) and augmented reality (AR) are also revolutionizing the way properties are marketed and sold. These technologies allow potential buyers to experience properties virtually, providing them with a realistic and immersive view of the space. The chapter discusses how real estate firms are using VR and AR to enhance the buying experience and reach a broader audience.

Blockchain technology is another game-changer in the real estate industry.

Blockchain offers a secure and transparent way to conduct transactions, reducing the risk of fraud and increasing trust among parties. The chapter explores the potential applications of blockchain in real estate, such as smart contracts, property title management, and digital identities.

    Moreover, technology is transforming property management and maintenance. The use of data analytics, Internet of Things (IoT) devices, and automation is enhancing the efficiency of property management, enabling real estate firms to monitor and manage properties in real-time. The chapter discusses how these technologies are improving operational efficiency, reducing costs, and enhancing tenant satisfaction.

10

Chapter 9: Navigating Economic Cycles

Economic cycles have a significant impact on both the tech and real estate industries. This chapter explores how organizations navigate economic downturns and capitalize on periods of economic growth. The chapter provides insights into the strategies and practices that help organizations remain resilient and thrive in different economic conditions.

During economic downturns, organizations must be agile and adaptable to navigate challenges and maintain stability. The chapter discusses how tech companies and real estate firms implement cost-saving measures, streamline operations, and focus on core competencies to weather economic storms. It also explores the importance of maintaining a long-term perspective and being prepared for economic fluctuations.

In periods of economic growth, organizations have the opportunity to expand and invest in new opportunities. The chapter explores how companies leverage economic growth to scale their operations, enter new markets, and drive innovation. It also discusses the importance of strategic planning and risk management in seizing growth opportunities.

Diversification is a key strategy for navigating economic cycles. Both tech companies and real estate firms recognize the importance of diversifying their portfolios to mitigate risks and enhance stability. The chapter explores how organizations diversify their revenue streams, investments, and markets to remain resilient in the face of economic uncertainties.

Moreover, this chapter examines the role of government policies and regulations in shaping economic cycles. Organizations must stay informed about policy changes and adapt their strategies accordingly. The chapter provides insights into how tech companies and real estate firms navigate regulatory environments and advocate for policies that support their growth and innovation.

11

Chapter 10: Sustainable and Ethical Practices

Sustainability and ethics are becoming increasingly important in both the tech and real estate industries. This chapter explores how organizations are adopting sustainable and ethical practices to create long-term value and contribute to a better world. The chapter discusses the benefits of sustainability and ethics, as well as the challenges organizations face in implementing these practices.

In the tech industry, sustainability initiatives focus on reducing the environmental impact of products and operations. The chapter explores how tech companies are developing energy-efficient technologies, reducing waste, and adopting renewable energy sources. It also discusses the role of corporate social responsibility (CSR) in driving sustainable practices and enhancing the reputation of tech companies.

The real estate industry also places a strong emphasis on sustainability. Sustainable building practices, such as green construction materials, energy-efficient designs, and renewable energy systems, are transforming the way properties are developed and managed. The chapter discusses how real estate firms are incorporating sustainability into their projects and the benefits it offers to the environment, tenants, and investors.

Ethical practices are equally important in both industries. The chapter explores how organizations are promoting transparency, fairness, and accountability in their operations. It discusses the importance of ethical leadership and the role of codes of conduct in guiding ethical behavior. The chapter also highlights the impact of ethical practices on building trust and maintaining positive relationships with stakeholders.

Furthermore, this chapter examines the challenges organizations face in implementing sustainable and ethical practices. From balancing short-term costs with long-term benefits to navigating regulatory requirements, organizations must overcome various obstacles to achieve their sustainability and ethics goals. The chapter provides insights into how successful companies address these challenges and create a positive impact.

12

Chapter 11: The Future of Work

The future of work is a topic of great interest in both the tech and real estate industries. This chapter explores the trends and developments shaping the future of work, such as remote work, flexible work arrangements, and the gig economy. The chapter discusses how organizations are adapting to these changes and the implications for employees, employers, and the broader economy.

Remote work has become a significant trend, driven by advancements in technology and changing employee preferences. The chapter explores how tech companies and real estate firms are embracing remote work and creating flexible work environments. It discusses the benefits of remote work, such as increased productivity, cost savings, and improved work-life balance, as well as the challenges, such as maintaining team cohesion and managing remote employees.

The gig economy is also transforming the way people work. The chapter discusses the rise of freelance and contract work, and how organizations are leveraging the gig economy to access specialized talent and enhance their workforce flexibility. It also explores the implications of the gig economy for workers, such as job security, benefits, and career development.

Moreover, this chapter examines the role of technology in shaping the future of work. From collaboration tools and virtual meeting platforms to artificial intelligence and automation, technology is transforming the way work is performed and managed. The chapter discusses how organizations are leveraging technology to enhance productivity, streamline processes, and create a more connected and efficient work environment.

The chapter also explores the importance of employee well-being and engagement in the future of work. Organizations recognize that happy and engaged employees are more productive and contribute to the overall success of the company. The chapter discusses how organizations are prioritizing employee well-being, offering wellness programs, and creating a positive work culture that fosters engagement and satisfaction.

13

Chapter 12: The Legacy of Pioneers

The final chapter reflects on the legacy of the pioneers of prosperity in both Silicon Valley and the real estate industry. It explores the lasting impact of their contributions on their industries, communities, and the world. The chapter discusses the lessons learned from their journeys and the lasting influence of their work.

The pioneers of Silicon Valley, with their relentless drive for innovation and excellence, have left an indelible mark on the world. Their contributions have not only transformed the tech industry but also revolutionized the way we live, work, and communicate. This chapter reflects on the enduring legacy of these visionaries and the lessons future generations can learn from their experiences.

Similarly, the real estate titans have reshaped urban landscapes and created iconic structures that stand as testaments to their vision and ingenuity. Their impact extends beyond the properties they have developed, influencing the way we think about urban planning, sustainability, and community development. The chapter explores the lasting contributions of these real estate moguls and their influence on the industry and society.

The chapter also highlights the importance of giving back and creating a positive impact on communities. Many of these pioneers have used their success to support philanthropic efforts, drive social change, and address global challenges. Their commitment to making a difference serves as an inspiration to others and underscores the importance of using one's influence for the greater good.

Moreover, this chapter emphasizes the role of mentorship and knowledge sharing in preserving the legacy of these pioneers. By passing on their wisdom and experiences to the next generation, these leaders ensure that their insights continue to inspire and guide future entrepreneurs. The chapter discusses the importance of fostering a culture of mentorship and the value of learning from those who have paved the way.

In conclusion, "Pioneers of Prosperity: Human Insights from Silicon Valley and Real Estate Leaders" provides a comprehensive exploration of the journeys, achievements, and impact of some of the most influential figures in these industries. Their stories offer valuable lessons in leadership, innovation, resilience, and the pursuit of excellence. As we look to the future, the insights and experiences of these pioneers will continue to inspire and guide us in our own endeavors, shaping the world for generations to come.

"Pioneers of Prosperity: Human Insights from Silicon Valley and Real Estate Leaders" takes you on a captivating journey through the lives of remarkable individuals who have shaped the worlds of technology and real estate. This book delves deep into the personal stories, challenges, and triumphs of Silicon Valley innovators and real estate moguls, uncovering the qualities and strategies that have driven their success. Through twelve engaging chapters, you will explore the principles of leadership, the power of innovation, and the importance of ethical practices in achieving long-term prosperity. This book not only celebrates individual achievements but also offers timeless insights and inspiration for anyone looking to make a significant impact in their field. Whether you're an aspiring entrepreneur, a seasoned professional, or simply curious about the forces driving these dynamic industries, "Pioneers of Prosperity" provides a wealth of knowledge and inspiration to guide you on your own path to success.

www.ingramcontent.com/pod-product-compliance
Lightning Source LLC
LaVergne TN
LVHW020742090526
838202LV00057BA/6183